It Is Always the Bad Guys

Rev. William Crumley CSC

OPTION Press

December, 2013

Dedication

I dedicate this book to Father Louis Brusatti. He is a member of the Faculty of Religious and Theological Studies at St. Edward's University in Austin, Texas.

It was his Sunday homily mentioned in chapter two of this book that inspired the format of this book. His homily was a series of questions which began: "Can you imagine?" As I listened I realized that rather than list a lot of facts which I would have to research and document I really needed to challenge the reader to imagine a better world.

Thank you, Father Lou!

INDEX

Preface — page i

Chapter 1 Globalization — page 1

Chapter 2 Imagining a better world — page 8

Chapter 3 The web of assassinations — page 17

Chapter 4 The disjointed society — page 26

Chapter 5 Economic aspects of war — page 43

Chapter 6 The perfect Nazi — page 60

Epilogue Restoring the common WEALTH — page 65

It Is Always the Bad Guys

PREFACE

The title came about at a session of a class "Borderlands" at St. Edwards University in Austin, Texas. I had been invited to teach one of the sessions. The students were to read a short paper entitled "Murder in Juarez". It described the murders (and in most cases sexual molestation) of young women who had taken jobs in garment factories of northern Mexico. After my talk I was invited to attend a two session video which explored the question on a deeper level. One of the obvious implications of the video is that local police and other authorities were doing little if anything to solve the murders. In their investigation officials were blaming the young women themselves and looking to blame gangs and other elements they considered less desirable elements of their society.

In a short discussion after the film the teacher asked for comments. I stated: "It's always the bad guys. They do not look at the elements of our society which lead to the killings. They try to find someone to blame so they can close the case." This is a pattern I have noticed in assassinations and other scandals in human history (cf. Chapter 3). As I watched the video I was very much aware that the same phenomena described in the video could occur in our own nation. I could envision young women in our own school burdened with the costs of their education seeking jobs that could lead them into difficult situations. As I left the video I picked up a new copy of the student newspaper. One of the articles on the front page was about a local student who took a job which placed her in a very difficult situation in which she was visually harassed by men old enough to be her father. She took the job only because she needed the money to help pay for her education.

I was also aware of a situation in an area I served as pastor for over twenty years. There was a garment factory which employed many young women – many of them mothers who needed to work in order to help support their families. One day I was approached by two men who hoped to organize a union. They were looking for potential leaders and persons who could help support their efforts. I suggested several names that might be helpful for them and told them I would be glad to support their efforts in any way I could. Several weeks later they came back and thanked me for my support. They also said that they were not going to proceed with their efforts. The officials of the garment factory had made it very clear that if an attempt was made to unionize the workers they would close the plant. Naturally, the workers would not attempt to organize under those conditions. Within months the factory was closed. A relatively new building with several abandoned trucks sits in a locked parking lot as a sign to any other group which would dare to organize workers to obtain better working conditions. My experience at St. Edwards University is described in chapter 1 of the book.

Over the years I have written two novels and a factual book on similar subjects. The first was <u>The Disjointed Society</u> a novel which describes the economic factors which underlie war and violence. The novel highlights the economic factors we fail to recognize when we consider the causes of war and violence. That novel is out of print. Then I wrote a factual book <u>Why We Are Always Broke: things we need to know about the economy</u>. This book documents the truth in the novel that I was capable of documenting. I completed a second novel <u>Restoring the Common WEALTH</u>. It contrasts a Native American model which looks at our real worth as our human life and the natural environment which sustains that life. It looks at all the elements in <u>Why We Are Always Broke</u> that I was able to verify and the elements I was not able to document. It is not necessary to footnote a novel.

My experience with the "Borderlands" class has led me to realize that I need to find the material for the parts of the novel I was not able to document and do a factual account which encompasses all the elements of <u>Restoring the Common WEALTH</u>. This book, <u>It Is Always The Bad Guys,</u> is that attempt. There are three parts to the book.

Part one highlights the choices we have and the choices we seem to prefer. Chapter 1 is a follow up on my talk to the "Borderlands" class. Chapter 2 is an alternative view. It looks at how Native Americans viewed the world before the introduction of "civilization". Chapter 3 deals with persons who have been murdered, including some of the victims of <u>Murder in Juarez</u>.

Part two deals with the forces which lead to war. Chapter 4 is "The Disjointed Society" it starts with a homily of Pope Victor 1, a character in <u>Restoring the Common Wealth</u>. He represents Pope John Paul 1. Many believe he was murdered. After the fictional homily the chapter contains material from the social teachings of popes from Leo XIII to John Paul II. Chapter 5 looks at the role of war, especially the economic aspects of war. Chapter 6 is called "The perfect Nazi". It looks at persons, organizations, and movements which reflect the dogmas and truths of Nazism even today.

Part three is "Restoring the Common WEALTH." It looks at individuals and movements which are helping people today to take a deeper look at our lives and our society. They do not simply accept a vision of history which ignores the interrelationship of historical events and simply places blame on the bad guys.

Chapter one Globalization

I began the class described in the preface of this book by asking several questions. WHAT IS A THIRD WORLD COUNTRY? Originally the term was applied to non-aligned nations. The first world was the nations of the North Atlantic Treaty Organizations (NATO), the second world referred to nations in the Soviet bloc, the third world was nations not aligned to either group. Eventually the "third world" came to be defined as any nation which was dependent on money and investment from the first world. Then a popular interpretation became the first world was Europe with its many colonies. The second world was the U.S.A. and the colonies it supported. The third world became countries supported economically by investments from Europe and the United States of America. Regardless of the interpretation you prefer, third world is a nation economically dependent on another nation.

Another question was IS MEXICO A THIRD WORLD NATION? The answer is yes. It is economically dependent. We need to change our concept of what it means to be economically dependent. Many nations originally defined as first or second world nations are now economically dependent. The U.S.A. is presently seventeen trillion dollars in debt. (1) Somewhere between 5% and 10% of that debt is owed to China. The majority of that money is owed to multinational banks in the form of interest and debt. National debts that plague so many nations are one effect of globalization.

So the next question is WHAT IS GLOBALIZATION? It is a many headed phenomenon. It is not something that has evolved only in recent years. It existed at least as early as 200 B.C. in what was known as the "silk road" that extended from China to northern Africa.

(1) We have lost a sense of what a trillion dollars is. If we spend a million dollars a day, we would only spend 525.6 billion dollars in a year. It would take almost 2 years to spend a trillion dollars, between 30 and 35 years to pay off our current national debt at the rate of a million dollars a day.

The "silk road" indicates how we are inclined to define history in terms of economic activity. The "silk road" did not include most of Europe, Africa south of what bordered on the Mediterranean Sea, or any of North or South America. These areas were "discovered" when European monetary interests found riches there that were profitable in commerce. With the development of modern transportation (e.g. railroads and steamships) modern globalization began to expand. The invention of the telephone, telegraph, and most recently the internet, has expanded globalization.

Some have given globalization a more benign interpretation. They define it as "compression" of the world through modern technology. This intensifies our consciousness of the world as a whole and gives a greater awareness of our interrelationship with the whole world. If this were the only effect of globalization it would certainly be positive. But we cannot remain blind to the economic effects of globalization. It is the economic effects we will consider in this book. In the year 2000 the International Monetary Fund identified four basic aspects of globalization: A) trade and commerce B) capital and investment C) migration of people D) dissemination of knowledge. (2) The elements of globalization as defined by the International Monetary Fund encompass both elements from the strictly economic definition and the more benign definition. However, the first two aspects are obviously economic. People do migrate because of persecution, but most migration is for economic reasons. Much knowledge disseminated has economic overtones. Almost all knowledge put out by the International Monetary Fund is economic knowledge. I raised the question DOES GLOBALIZATION CREATE MORE THIRD WORLD COUNTRIES OR LESS THIRD WORLD COUNTRIES? The U.S. Agency for International Development says for every dollar invested in Latin America three dollars leaves that country.

(2) Cf. Wikipedia: Globalization

If that is true, then globalization is creating more third world nations not less. The irony is that the three dollars which leave the third world goes to private corporations. The U.S. Government is becoming ever more indebted.

The borderlands class began with an account of several young unmarried girls who were murdered near Juarez, Mexico. The ones described were unmarried and under twenty years old. July 17, 1995 a 17 year old girl disappeared. Her body was found 2 months later. February 1999 a 13 year old girl was sent home from work. Her body was found in a drainage canal. September 2001 a 19 year old girl who was a student disappeared. The next month a 20 year old woman arrived at work four minutes late. The door of the *maquiladora* where she worked was closed. She never returned home. In November 2001 these two were found in a shallow grave along with six other women. All 8 had been raped and strangled! By mid-2002 an estimated three hundred women had been murdered and more women were missing. Most of the women were young slender women with long black hair AND THEY WERE POOR. In the first 9 months of 1998 women in Juarez reported 800 cases of rape and over 9000 cases of violence, including rape, kidnapping, and domestic violence.

We might think this is a problem only for Mexico and other "third world" country. It certainly is a problem for other "third world" nations as is indicated from this account of Bangladesh indicates: "I was up at dawn one morning in Dhaka, Bangladesh to see a remarkable sight: thousands of people walking to work in long lines stretching from the outskirts of Dhaka and from some of its poorest neighborhoods. Looking more closely, I noticed that these workers were almost all young women, perhaps between the age of 18 and 25. They are the workers of a burgeoning garment industry in Dhaka who cut, stitch, and package millions of pieces of apparel each month for shipment to the United States and Europe.

Over the years, I have visited garment factories all over the developing world. ... There is nothing glamorous about this work. The women often walk two hours each morning in long quiet files to get to work. Arriving at seven or seven-thirty, they may be in their seats for most of the following twelve hours. They often work with no break at all or perhaps a very short lunch break, with little chance to go to the lavatory. Leering bosses lean over them, posing a threat of sexual harassment. After a long, difficult, tedious day, the young women trudge back home, where they are sometimes threatened with physical assault. (emphasis added)

How is this different from the account described in "Murder in Juarez"? Somehow the author, Mr. Sachs overlooks the fact that the exploitation he describes can be corrected. He continues in the very next paragraph:

"These sweatshop jobs are the targets of public protest in developed countries: those protests have helped to improve the safety and quality of the working conditions. The rich-world protestors, however, should support increased numbers of such jobs, albeit under safer working conditions, by protesting the trade protectionism in their own countries that keep out garment exports from countries such as Bangladesh. These young women already have a foothold in the modern economy that is a critical, measurable step up from the villages." (3)

That was the rationale that some people used to push NAFTA. Later on page 50 of The <u>End of Poverty</u> it is clear Mr. Sachs does not understand the underlying problem (the greed of corporations). For Sachs the problem is poverty. He does not view poverty as a symptom but as a cause. The cause is greed. He says: "Poor rural villages lack trucks, paved roads, power generators, irrigation channels." (3)

Jeffrey Sachs, <u>The End of Poverty</u>   p. 11

What he doesn't say is they also lack jobs. He also says: "natural capital is depleted, the trees have been cut down and the soil nutrients exhausted." But who has cut down the trees and exhausted the natural nutrients of the earth? THE CORPORATIONS! And WHY? TO MAKE A PROFIT! (4)

Is this a problem in the USA? The student newspaper <u>Hilltop Views</u> at St. Edward's University in Austin, Texas describes a unique job a student pays to help offset the cost of her education. She has taken a job as a model at a car show. So far she has not been forced to model nude but is fearful that she may be forced to do that. She describes men old enough to be her father visually harassing her. She is fearful this may affect her future. (5) She has not had the problem the young women in Mexico have had. However, the underlying reason is the same - corporations using any attempt necessary to make a profit.

What are the causes of this problem? "By analyzing the crime scene in Juarez, Mexico one can deduce that the sexualized murder suggests anger at the increasing sexual independence of young women in Mexico. The mutilated breasts suggest anger at women's use of their bodies for more than mothering and nurturing. The women are primarily working women suggesting resentment at women's increasing economic independence. Abandonment of their bodies in the desert like garbage reveals that these women are considered cheap and disposable. What is not apparent at the crime scene is the class hierarchy – embedded in global capitalism and expressed through gender – that plays an integral part in these murders.

(4) Ibid. p. 50

(5) St. Edward's University Hilltop Views Wednesday November 14, 2013; p. 1

Economic restructuring in the last two decades has created a new international division of labor that particularly exploits women in third world countries. Necessary to this division has been the construction of female labor as cheap and disposable when paradoxically, global capitalism depends upon these women to assemble its commodities. WHILE MULTINATIONAL CORPORATIONS PROFIT FROM THE *MAQUILADORAS* IN JUAREZ, THE MURDERED WOMEN AND THEIR FAMILIES BEAR THE COST OF GLOBAL CAPITALISM." (6) (EMPHASIS ADDED)

What are the causes? The causes are Macho backlash due to women taking men's jobs, globalization – global corporations coming into to a poor country to get cheap labor   NAFTA – North American Free Trade Agreement. Is this something new for Mexico?

"Rieber was among those, like Davis, who had high hopes for Juan Almazan's bid for the Mexican presidency to succeed in favor of the Axis. On February 12, 1940, the American Embassy in Mexico City reported that Texas Oil of Arizona (Davis' company) was working in close collusion with affiliated oil groups including Davis Oil Company in directing the clandestine entry of arms into Mexico. The arms were to support a possible military coup by Almazan in the event of his defeat at the polls."

The American Embassy report stated: "Oil Company secret service operatives are ridiculing the Mexican Government for the glass-eyed vigilance on the border, as they call it, that enables them to execute adroit introduction of arms without detection."

---

(6) <u>Murder in Juarez: Gender, Sexual Violence, and the Global Assembly Line</u> P.70 and Fronntiers/2001 Vol. 25 No. 1

The report also adds: "I find that large sums of oil money are being paid out on the border for protection and I have also ascertained that Custom House officials on the American side of the line at Eagle Pass, Texas have accepted money to facilitate the departure of arms from the U.S.A. through this American port of entry." (emphasis added) (7)

This network established ten months before the USA entered World War Two as an enemy of Hitler was used during WW2 as a tool to supply Hitler with arms and planes. Mr. Rieber was chairman of Texas Oil Company (Texaco). His company and Davis Oil Company continued to supply the Nazis during WW2. They used Mexico as one of the countries that enabled them to avoid the blockade imposed by the US Government. U.S. Corporations using Mexico and other 3rd world countries to make a profit did not start with NAFTA.

7. In 1983 Charles Higham wrote a book <u>Trading With The Enemy: An Expose' of the Nazi-American Money Plot 1933-1949.</u> The above quote is from page 77 of that book.

Chapter 2 Can you imagine?

The priest began his homily with a whole series of questions saying "Can you imagine ...?" You can fill in any series of human events which the priest was challenging his listeners to imagine – a world without war, people taking care of one another, Israel and Palestine living in harmony. The first step in the realization of that dream is for a number of people to dream the dream, imagine the unimaginable. Ghandi could imagine a world which Hindu and Moslem could live together. Kennedy could imagine a western hemisphere where North America and South America could become partners. King could imagine a USA in which black children and white children could walk together hand and hand. He could also imagine a world without war. His most famous speech contained a whole series of dreams he could dream, visions he could envision.

The fulfillment of a dream or an imagined goal has to come about when someone begins to set up the structures to fulfill that dream. Unfortunately once the dreamer is no longer present the dream can become distorted. The next chapter will show the effect on many dreams when the dreamer is no longer present. This chapter will look simply at the dream of the dreamers.

The original Native Americans were not "civilized". They had this weird idea that no one could own the resources of the earth. They existed for the benefit of all creation. They were to be used for the good of all of creation. Any use of these resources which hindered the good of ALL creation was not acceptable. If I read it correctly this "weird" idea of common ownership of the land is the first idea expressed in the Judeo-Christian Bible. In that account the world was created. Human beings were charged with protecting the water, the earth, the air, the land, the trees, the heat and light of the sun. These elements were (supposedly still ARE) our common WEALTH.

Only when they became "civilized" did the sons and daughters of Adam and Eve come to believe that they could actually own these elements, control these elements, and use them in any way they wish. Maybe that is the most basic "Can you imagine" - all of creation being used only for the good of all creation. That would not be a new imagined species. Someone had to imagine such a creation for it to appear in <u>Genesis</u>. Some Native Americans imagined it and lived it for many centuries. It is only when human beings were "civilized" that someone's dream was distorted. To rephrase our most basic imagination: imagine a de-civilized (not uncivilized) universe. G. K. Chesterton once said: "Christianity has not been tried and found wanting, Christianity has been found difficult and has not been tried." Someone's dream has been found difficult and not been tried.

Ghandi was an advocate of nonviolence. In his promotion of nonviolence he realized that in order to be nonviolent sometimes it was necessary to disobey the law. He was a lawyer. He had studied law. He realized that laws were made by mortals. Law could be and often was unjust. Being nonviolent sometimes required that a person or a group be disobedient to the law. He was arrested in his life because of his disobedience to the law. The English colonized his home nation of India. They declared that only English corporations could manufacture salt. Ghandi led a group of citizens of India to the sea to manufacture salt in direct defiance to the English order. Eventually his nonviolence predominated and English was forced to grant independence to India.

Some of Ghandi's more famous quotes show his nonviolent character and the basic philosophy of his life: "Seven social sins: politics without principles, wealth without work, pleasure without conscience, knowledge without character, commerce without morality, science without humanity, and worship without sacrifice."

"I came to the conclusion long ago ... that all religions were true and also that all had some error in them, and whilst I hold by my own, I should hold others as dear as Hinduism. So we can only pray, if we are Hindus, not that a Christian should become a Hindu ... But our innermost prayer should be a Hindu should be a better Hindu, a Muslim a better Muslim, a Christian a better Christian."

"I am not a visionary. I claim to be a practical idealist. The religion of nonviolence is not meant merely for the Rishis and saints. It is meant for the common people as well. Nonviolence is the law of our species as violence is the law of the brute. The spirit lies dormant in the brute and he knows no law but that of physical might. The dignity of man requires obedience to a higher law — to the strength of the spirit."

"If we are to reach real peace in this world and if we are to carry on a real war against war, we shall have to begin with children; and if they will grow up in their natural innocence, we won't have to struggle, we won't have to pass fruitless idle resolutions. But we shall go from love to love and peace to peace, until at last all the corners of the world are covered with that peace and love for which, consciously or unconsciously, the whole world is hungering."

"We cannot evoke the true spirit of sacrifice and valour, so long as we are not free. I know the British Government will not be able to withhold freedom from us, when we have made enough self-sacrifice. We must, therefore, purge ourselves of hatred."

"Ours is not a drive for power, but purely a non-violent fight for India's independence. In a violent struggle, a successful general has been often known to effect a military coup and to set up a dictatorship. But under the Congress scheme of things, essentially non-violent as it is, there can be no room for dictatorship. A non-violent soldier of freedom will covet nothing for himself, he fights only for the freedom of his country." (1)

(1) Quotes from Ghandi could be found in many places. These we found at Wikiquote Mahatma Ghandi http://en.wikiquote.org/wiki/Mahatma_Gandhi

In March 1961 President John Kennedy announced the establishment of the Alliance for Progress. The announced purpose of the Alliance was to bring peace, progress, and prosperity to the sovereign nations of Central and South America. President Kennedy spoke of all American nations as a single entity when he announced the Alliance to a group of Latin American diplomats and members of Congress on March 13, 1961.

"The living standards of every American family will be on the rise, basic education will be available to all, hunger will be a forgotten experience, the need for massive outside help will have passed, most nations will have entered a period of self-sustaining growth, and, although there will be still much to do, every American Republic will be the master of its own revolution and its own hope and progress." (2)

Kennedy continued: "Let me stress that only the most determined efforts of the American nations themselves can bring success to this effort. They, and they alone, can mobilize their resources, enlist the energies of their people, and modify their social patterns so that all, and not just a privileged few, share in the fruits of growth. If this effort is made, then outside assistance will give a vital impetus to progress; without it, no amount of help will advance the welfare of the people." (3)

President Kennedy announced that he requested $500 million from Congress to help kick off this program. "The money will be used to combat illiteracy, improve the productivity and use of their land, wipe out disease, attack archaic tax and land-tenure structures, provide educational opportunities, and offer a broad range of projects designed to make the benefits of increasing abundance available to all. We will begin to commit these funds as soon as they are appropriated." (4)

(2) **Address by President Kennedy at a White House Reception for Latin American Diplomats and Members of Congress, March 13, 1961** paragraph 6 as noted in http://www.fordham.edu/halsall/mod/1961kennedy-afp1.html

(3) **Ibid.** paragraph 7   (4) **Ibid.** paragraph 10

Kennedy mentioned a planned meeting of the Inter-American Economic and Social Council. He announced a seven part program which he hoped the alliance would foster.

support for economic integration among Inter-American nations

stabilize economic prices so less money is drained out of other American nations

increase the food for peace program

expand the education efforts in other American nations

train persons to monitor economies in other American nations

work for greater peace in American nations so that monies now diverted to war can be diverted to meet needs of the people.

send U.S. students to other American nations to learn your values and traditions (5)

Kennedy ended his speech: "And so I say to the men and women of the Americas - to the [peasant] in the fields, to the *obrero* [worker] in the cities, to the *estudiante* in the schools - prepare your mind and heart for the task ahead, call forth your strength, and let each devote his energies to the betterment of all so that your children and our children in this hemisphere can find an ever richer and a freer life.

Let us once again transform the American Continent into a vast crucible of revolutionary ideas and efforts, a tribute to the power of the creative energies of free men and women, an example to all the world that liberty and progress walk hand in hand. Let us once again awaken our American revolution until it guides the struggles of people everywhere-not with an imperialism of force or fear but the rule of courage and freedom and hope for the future of man." (6) Why would so lofty a goal fail? Varied reasons have been given for its failure. One reason asserted for its failure is that it was not really an effort to develop Latin America. It was simply a tool to prevent the rise of communism in the Americas. The Bay of Pigs operation and the Cuban Missile Crisis simply fostered that interpretation.

(5) Ibid. paragraphs 11-18   (6) Ibid. paragraphs 25-26

With the murder of Kennedy and the escalation of the war in Vietnam, focus in Latin America shifted from development of the people to keeping the communists out. Latin American nations were coerced into boycotting Cuba. By the time Richard Nixon became president the Alliance was virtually dead. The flow of drugs into the USA became a more serious problem. Little attention was paid to the role of the CIA and other U.S. entities in this problem. All these phenomena helped to destroy the Alliance for Progress.

A good analysis of the Alliance for Progress is found in the following: "Fifty years later, the Alliance for Progress provides a valuable lesson for the U.S. Washington needs to stay focused on the region's real threats: land rights, employment, and government accountability. With the drug war, the U.S. is falling into the same trap as it did in the 1960s—spending on a futile war, exacerbating regional violence, and putting already-corrupt institutions into unwinnable quagmires. It's time for a new Alliance for Progress, but this time, it needs to stay true to Kennedy's original vision of economic and social justice for all Americans, not just those living in the U.S." (7)

One of the clearest non-violent aims of Martin Luther King is expressed in this presentation:

"Along with the march as a weapon for change in our nonviolent arsenal must be listed the boycott. Basic to the philosophy of nonviolence is the refusal to cooperate with evil. There is nothing quite so effective as a refusal to cooperate economically with the forces and institutions which perpetuate evil in our communities.

(7) "Alliance for Progress" Still a Noble Goal in Latin America found in "World Policy Blog" September 20, 2011 http://www.worldpolicy.org/blog/2011/09/20/alliance-progress-still-noble-goal-latin-america

In the past six months simply by refusing to purchase products from companies which do not hire Negroes in meaningful numbers and in all job categories, the Ministers of Chicago under SCLC's Operation Breadbasket have increased the income of the Negro community by more than two million dollars annually. In Atlanta the Negroes' earning power has been increased by more than twenty million dollars annually over the past three years through a carefully disciplined program of selective buying and negotiations by the Negro minister. This is nonviolence at its peak of power, when it cuts into the profit margin of a business in order to bring about a more just distribution of jobs and opportunities for Negro wage earners and consumers.

But again, the boycott must be sustained over a period of several weeks and months to assure results. This means continuous education of the community in order that support can be maintained. People will work together and sacrifice if they understand clearly why and how this sacrifice will bring about change. We can never assume that anyone understands. It is our job to keep people informed and aware.

Our most powerful nonviolent weapon is, as would be expected, also our most demanding, that is organization. To produce change, people must be organized to work together in units of power. These units might be political, as in the case of voters' leagues and political parties; they may be economic units such as groups of tenants who join forces to form a tenant union or to organize a rent strike; or they may be laboring units of persons who are seeking employment and wage increases.

More and more, the civil rights movement will become engaged in the task of organizing people into permanent groups to protect their own interests and to produce change in their behalf. This is a tedious task which may take years, but the results are more permanent and meaningful.

In the future we will be called upon to organize the unemployed, to unionize the business within the ghetto, to bring tenants together into collective bargaining units and establish cooperatives for purposes of building viable financial institutions within the ghetto that can be controlled by Negroes themselves.

There is no easy way to create a world where men and women can live together, where each has his own job and house and where all children receive as much education as their minds can absorb. But if such a world is created in our lifetime, it will be done in the United States by Negroes and white people of good will. It will be accomplished by persons who have the courage to put an end to suffering by willingly suffering themselves rather than inflict suffering upon others. It will be done by rejecting the racism, materialism and violence that has characterized Western civilization and especially by working toward a world of brotherhood, cooperation and peace." (8)

Ghandi, Kennedy, King and others were trying to help create structures which would promote non-violence and help ordinary people become more economically self-sufficient. Meanwhile those in control of the money were generating wars and economic conflicts. With the end of each of the major world wars international banks were set up. These banks controlled the flow of money internationally. They also controlled the flow of information which was used worldwide in making economic decisions.

The dreams of the dreamers were distorted and eventually destroyed. Through the banks they created money based on debt began to replace money based on work. In the process money no longer stays in a local community and turns over several times in that community.

---

(8) Nonviolence: The Only Road to Freedom *Martin Luther King, Jr.* May 04, 1966 as quoted in TeachingAmericanHistory.org
http://teachingamericanhistory.org/library/document/nonviolence-the-only-road-to-freedom/

Very little money actually remains in a local community. Very little is actually generated in a local community. One of the common hopes expressed by Ghandi, Kennedy, and King was that local communities would become more self-sustaining. That aim is now overcome by globalization.

When I was a child we had a saying "we are cheap around here. We buy from one another." One possible meaning of the word "cheap" is stingy. As a child I always took that as the meaning of "cheap" in this saying. Only in recent years have I begun to appreciate the statement we used as children. It is much cheaper to buy from one another. Each dollar spent turns over several times in a local community. Each dollar will purchase several different items. It is much cheaper to buy from one another. Today we are forced in globalization. We will look at the effects of that globalization in a later chapter. The next chapter will look at the assassinations of some prominent persons who resisted this flow of money.

Chapter 3 The web of assassinations

Assassinations listed in Wikipedia date from 1200 B.C. The site lists nearly 700 assassinations in the last fifty years. These are only the assassinations of prominent persons. It would not include the murders of the young women in Mexico who were mentioned in the first chapter of this book. Only about 11% of assassinations name any convicted assassin. (1) If we believe we have a responsibility to convict assassins we are not doing a very good job.

I recently read a book Web of Debt by Ellen Hogsdon Brown. I was intrigued by the title and looked up "web" in the dictionary. I found three definitions which seemed to fit what the author described in her book: 1) a carefully woven trap or snare 2) a complicated work of the mind 3) an intricacy of pattern, interconnectedness of elements.

A web requires someone or something to spin the web, a web spinner. I found this definition of web spinner: "an order of small, secretive, tropical and subtropical insects that live in silk lined tunnels underground." Debt and murder are not the work of tropical and subtropical insects. They are created by human beings. Many persons who have been assassinated were challenging unjust economic systems. Someone was making a lot of money through this unjust system. Someone was living in a silk lined tunnel. In regard to the assassination they were underground.

As I mentioned in the preface of this book I wrote a book: Why We Are Always Broke: things we need to know about the economy. A friend of mine told me one day: "If you want to know why something happens, follow the money trail." I could see some truth to his statement. However, his statement seemed to me to be too simplistic. I began my research in order to prove him wrong.

1. Cf. Wikipedia List of Assassinations

As I got deeper and deeper into the money trail I realized that it was much broader than I would ever have imagined. I also realized that the money trail was controlled by only a few people and institutions. These people and institutions created a web of debt. A web is defined as a carefully woven trap or snare. It can also be defined as a complicated work of the mind. A common ingredient of web is intricacy of pattern and interconnectedness of elements. A web is usually created with some form of conspiracy. One definition of conspiracy is: "planning or acting together secretly especially for an unlawful or harmful purpose such as treason or murder." There are three common elements in web spinning and conspiracy. The activity is secret, it is unlawful, it occurs underground and someone profits from it and lives in a silk lined tunnel. Conspiracy occurs BEFORE the unlawful or harmful event (e.g. murder) takes place. It is normally not carried out by the ones who plan the conspiracy.

It is not easy to prove conspiracy because usually the conspirators are nowhere to be seen when the actual conspiratorial event takes place. The only person ever tried for the murder of John F. Kennedy was Clay Shaw. He was acquitted. At the time of Kennedy's murder he was in California. He was not in Dallas where the murder took place or in New Orleans when the conspiracy allegedly took place. Every other member of the alleged conspiracy was dead. The New Orleans District Attorney was unable to subpoena witnesses from outside of his jurisdiction. So he could not subpoena any witnesses from Dallas where the murder took place. It was an impossible task to prove any form of conspiracy. Eventually the movie "JFK" was filmed. The movie took a new look at John Kennedy's assassination. A lengthy scene in the movie depicts the New Orleans District Attorney, Jim Garrison, meeting with a man who will only identify himself as "Mr. X" who encourages Garrison to pursue his investigation because he is the only person who is pursuing the case.

"Mr. X" tells Garrison that he needs to pursue the question "WHY" Kennedy was killed. The most anyone else has pursued is "WHO" killed Kennedy and "HOW" he was killed. For a true understanding of the case we need to pursue "WHY" he was killed. This is very common among investigations of assassinations. We look at the "who" and the "how" but rarely the "why".

Several years ago a close friend of mine Father Vince O'Connell died. One day he told me about a conspiracy to kill him. Father Vince had worked tirelessly to help bring strawberry workers and small strawberry growers together in the same union which would help all of them obtain greater economic independence and security. In this case large corporate interests prevailed. The emerging union was sued. The judge ruled that the union was unconstitutional because it brought together labor and management in the same union. The union leaders were given suspended sentences but were forbidden to engage in any form of union activity the rest of their lives and the union was fined to the full extent of its treasury.

Pressure was put on Father O'Connell's religious community to transfer him out of the state in which the union activity took place. He was transferred from the deep-south to Minneapolis, Minnesota. One day he was driving in Minneapolis. A car pulled up alongside of him and fired several shots at him. Fortunately the shots missed. Vince followed the car and was able to run it off the road. He found a good Irish policeman who was horrified when he saw Vince in his Roman collar. The policeman was deeply in debt. He needed money quickly and was told to kill someone. He was given a car description of his victim and told where he might find that victim. If we look only at who pulls the shots we will see no pattern, no form of conspiracy. When we look at murders (e.g. John Kennedy) we look only at who pulls the trigger.

Most people who try to prove JFK was killed by conspiracy try to prove more than one gunman. Two, three, or more gunmen do not prove conspiracy. Each could have acted alone. Even if they were hired by the same person or group they may not have known each other or know that others were hired to do the killing.

This chapter of <u>It Is Always The Bad Guys</u> is not going to consider who did the actual murder. It will look at the various victims, what they did, and what was the effect of their activity. The material cited in this chapter should demonstrate an intricacy of pattern and interconnectedness and demonstrate an order of secretive persons or groups who figuratively live in silk lined tunnels underground.

If we look at the victims of assassinations listed in Wikipedia we find a large portion of these victims were heads of state, religious leaders, writers and others who spoke out strongly and/or acted against social (and most often economic) injustice. Opposing them were individuals and groups who made considerable money as a result of the unjust economic system.

The first United States President to be murdered was Abraham Lincoln. He was reputedly murdered because of his stance against slavery. Slavery was an economic issue as well as a social and moral issue. What we have not been told in regard to his murder was that Lincoln attempted to place and to keep the control of United States money in the hands of the Federal Government. In order to pay government expenses from the Civil War Lincoln had created the "greenbacks". The "greenbacks" were created because the bankers tried to charge the U.S. Government interest ranging 24% to 36% on money borrowed by the Government to fund the Civil War. Lincoln decided it would be cheaper for the Government to create its own money.

This was the same "mistake" John Kennedy made in 1963. Kennedy issued presidential order 11110 in early June 1963. This order restored the printing of the "silver certificate" which was U. S. money backed by silver and gold. Within a few hours of his death this process stopped. No presidential or congressional order ended the process. The silver certificates simply passed from existence. No investigation into the death of John Kennedy ever looked at this action as a possible motivation for his death. The person alleged to be his murderer was gunned down publicly and never brought to trial.

Another important person assassinated in the United States was the brother of President Kennedy, Robert Kennedy. He had just won the presidential primary in California. There was a good chance he would win the presidential nomination in a few months. There was a very good chance he would be the next president of the United States. He never got a chance to celebrate his California victory. Immediately after his victory speech he was shot as he left the podium where he acknowledged victory. He died within hours. He had promised to end United States involvement in the war in Vietnam. He had hinted that he would re-open the investigation into John Kennedy's death. He was certainly a threat to the same people who hated his murdered brother. His killer was tried as a person mentally deranged. He still sits in prison forty five years after the murder of Robert Kennedy. Many reports of the murder indicate that there were more shots fired than could have been fired by a lone gunman. This is also true of the murder of John Kennedy.

In the murder of John Kennedy the apparently fatal bullet came from the front. Other shots came from the rear. This would seem to indicate at least two gunmen. The only trial which looked at the possibility of more than one gunman (in fact, the only trial directly involving John Kennedy's murder) was the Clay Shaw trial in New Orleans. As was indicated above none of the major witnesses were alive. District Attorney Garrison had no jurisdiction to subpoena witnesses and document what might substantiate his case.

James Earl Ray pleaded guilty to the murder of Martin Luther King. He never stood trial for King's murder. He received a 99 year prison sentence. Ray later retracted his guilty plea and asked for a trial. That trial never came. The family of Martin Luther King believed that James Earl Ray was not the one who fired the fatal shot at Martin Luther King. The family was able to obtain a trial for Loyd Jowers for the assassination of Doctor King. The jury agreed with the family. The transcript of the trial shows the following:

THE COURT: I have authorized this gentleman here to take one picture of you which I'm going to have developed and make copies and send to you as I promised. Okay. All right, ladies and gentlemen. Let me ask you, do all of you agree with this verdict?

THE JURY: Yes (in unison).

THE COURT: In answer to the question did Loyd Jowers participate in a conspiracy to do harm to Dr. Martin Luther King, your answer is yes. Do you also find that others, including governmental agencies, were parties to this conspiracy as alleged by the defendant? Your answer to that one is also yes. And the total amount of damages you find for the plaintiffs entitled to is one hundred dollars. Is that your verdict? THE JURY: Yes (in unison).

That trial received little media publicity. However, this account of the trial does survive: "This historic trial was so ignored by the media that, apart from the courtroom participants, I was the only person who attended it from beginning to end. What I experienced in that courtroom ranged from inspiration at the courage of the Kings, their lawyer-investigator William F. Pepper, and the witnesses, to amazement at the government's carefully interwoven plot to kill Dr. King. The seriousness with which US intelligence agencies planned the murder of Martin Luther King, Jr. speaks eloquently of the threat King and nonviolence represented to the powers that be in the spring of 1968." (2)

(2) Jim Douglass The King Trial originally reported in Fellowship of Reconciliation Magazine and quoted in Wikipedia under Loyd Jowers.

The New York Times archives lists this story of Loyd Jowers' death: Loyd Jowers, the former Memphis cafe owner who maintained that he had hired someone other than James Earl Ray to assassinate the Rev. Dr. Martin Luther King Jr., died on Saturday at a hospital in this northwest Tennessee town. He was 73 and lived in nearby Tiptonville.

Mr. Jowers had lung cancer and had recently suffered a heart attack, said his lawyer, Lewis K. Garrison.

Mr. Jowers ran a cafe on the ground floor of a rooming house from which prosecutors say a sniper fired the shot that killed Dr. King on April 4, 1968. Mr. Ray confessed to the killing in 1969 but recanted and spent the rest of his life trying to prove his innocence. He died in prison in 1998.

In an ABC television interview in 1993, Mr. Jowers said he had received $100,000 from a Memphis produce merchant, Frank Liberto, to arrange Dr. King's murder. Mr. Liberto had died by the time of the interview, in which Mr. Jowers said that he had hired the assassin and that it was not Mr. Ray. (3)

In the assassination of Martin Luther King there was no trial of his confessed assassin. The confessed assassin, James Earl Ray, later retracted his confession but was never allowed a trial. William F. Pepper (attorney for the King family) maintains that he knows who killed Martin Luther King (and it wasn't James Earl Ray) and has the evidence and proof to substantiate his claims. However, civil authorities will not allow him to re-open the case. (4)

Was Salvador Allende assassinated? Or did he commit suicide? He was unquestionably run from office. He died as a result of that removal from office. There was no immediate trial or investigation into how his death came about. The military junta which took over the government ruled that Allende had committed suicide.

(3) Cf.http://www.nytimes.com/2000/05/23/us/loyd-jowers-73-who-claimed-a-role-in-the-killing-of-dr-king.html

(4) Cf. YouTube presentation of William Pepper. He also is working with Sirhan Sirhan whom he also maintains was not the murderer of Robert Kennedy. http://www.youtube.com/watch?v=8ISfWE6dMgw

This was for many years the "official" and only version of his death. Many followers claimed he was assassinated. His family members have publicly agreed with the suicide interpretation of his death. In late January, 2011 over thirty eight years after his death a Chilean court ruled that Allende's death was by suicide. This seemed to settle the case. However, May 31 of that same year Chilean TV reported that a 300 page document had been found in a home destroyed in an earthquake in Chile in 2010. That document led two forensic experts who examined it to believe that Allende die by murder not by suicide.

Whether we look at the assassination of Abraham Lincoln, John Kennedy, Robert Kennedy, Martin Luther King or Salvador Allende we find similar accounts of their individual deaths. They are involved in similar kind of activity. All are trying to create a more just society. All are in a position to help create that more just society. In working to create that more just society, all have built up strong opponents who have the ability to destroy them. These opponents control much of the flow of money. In only one of these five cases did the one alleged to be the assassin actually stand trial. That was Sirhan Sirhan in the assassination of Robert Kennedy. Attorneys for Sirhan are now claiming that he was framed and new evidence shows that at least thirteen bullets were fired at Robert Kennedy's assassination. The gun used by Sirhan Sirhan could only fire eight bullets without reloading. New evidence seems to indicate the fatal shots were fired behind Robert Kennedy. Sirhan stood in front of Kennedy. As the movie "JFK" points out: investigation looks at the "who" and the "how" of the assassination but neglects looking at the "why". That is, perhaps, the most common pattern in assassinations.

Another important assassination is that of Archbishop Oscar Romero of El Salvador. Romero was gunned down as he said mass on March 24, 1980. There were many priests and religious murdered in El Salvador at the time of Archbishop Romero.

When he was appointed Archbishop many residents of El Salvador presumed that he would not take any serious stands against the ruling government. Many religious leaders who were developing base communities and promoting liberation theology assumed the Archbishop would attempt to hinder their efforts. Somehow he did not follow that path. He began to speak out loudly and clearly at the social injustices he saw. At one point Archbishop Romero wrote to U.S. President Jimmie Carter and asked that he give no more monetary to El Salvador because that money was being used against the people of El Salvador.

Some U.S.A. assassinations mentioned above brought a conviction that many questioned and continue to question today. In some cases there was no trial. Like President Kennedy the federal government never tried anyone for the murder of Archbishop Romero. This failure may supply us with the clue we need in order to solve these murders.

Regarding Romero's murder someone said: "What the people of El Salvador need is for the murderer(s) of Archbishop Romero to be tried, to be convicted, and to be forgiven." It is interesting the person did not say that the murderer(s) need(s) to be forgiven. (S)He said the people of El Salvador need to forgive. The people of El Salvador need to be faithful to the vision of the creator. Maybe we need to give the creator's imaginings a try. Our vision, our imagination certainly is not working. The unsolved murders stem from a human imagination that has failed. Imagine a world in which we knew whom we need to forgive so that we can go about the business of forgiving them and get on with work envisioned by the creator. That same work was envisioned by the assassination victims. As long as we spend our energies trying to solve the assassinations we do not feel compelled to go about the work of those victims in creating a more just world. Like the people of El Salvador we need the real assassins to be tried, convicted, and forgiven so that we might freely pursue the vision and direction of their lives.

Chapter 4 The disjointed society

The previous chapter looked at some of the more notorious assassinations in our lifetime. Some people died mysteriously and the death has never been fully examined. One of these persons was Pope John Paul 1. He simply did not wake up one morning. There have been allegations that he was murdered. Books have been written. Plays have been produced. There has even been a movie which makes that claim. Two novels I wrote make that claim. The title of this chapter is taken from the title of that first novel, "The Disjointed Society". In the second novel Pope Victor 1 (used as an image of the real Pope John Paul 1) gives a homily. This chapter will repeat that homily and conclude with real material presented by two real Popes (Leo XIII and his encyclical <u>Rerum Novarum</u> and John Paul II and his encyclical <u>Centesimus Annus</u>).

"We live in a disjointed society. We have managed to destroy most of our basic relationships. We have broken up families and family ties. We have pulverized neighborhoods so that one neighbor does not know another. We have made the local merchant a thing of the past. In his place we have created the global village.

A global village is the best political and economic structure we can create if that global village is based on the truth that we are a single people that are bound together as intimately as the people of a remote third world village. But the global village being created is NOT based on our common humanity. Instead a few persons of greed are trying to exploit other residents of the global village - especially the poorest.

Instead of building a global village based on the diversity of people who make up that village, it is being built on the premise that everyone must conform. We look for the least common denominator of our humanity which deprives us of our humanity, our individuality, our freedom as well as our sense of dignity and worth. Instead of being joined together we are becoming even more disjointed.

We are separating realities which need to be joined. We separate the worker and the product of his work. We separate jurisdiction and responsibility. How often do we hold those in positions of power responsible for their acts? We even manage to separate ourselves from reality. Reality, for us, is nuclear war. Over a trillion dollars a year are spent on arms. That amounts to five thousand dollars a year for every poor person in the world. A poor family of six persons could receive thirty thousand dollars a year based on their share of the money spent in a year on arms. We certainly have separated ourselves from reality. We have separated ourselves from history. We do not look back on some of the great civilizations of the past and recognize that they disappeared not because a stronger force came and overpowered them. Rather, they disintegrated from within. Often that disintegration was the result of a moral corruption. Their religious practices were built on ritual and superstition, not faith.

We do not look at how the Russians were able to destroy Napoleon by submitting passively to him. They allowed him to take as much of Russia as he desired. Napoleon's own greed was his downfall. He wanted more and more of Russia. However, he could not feed his own army. So, he was forced to retreat in shame. We fail to look at Louis XIV and the causes of the French Revolution. France was so busy trying to defend herself and her vast empire that there was no money to take care of the basic needs of the people. And so, Louis XIV fell.

We also have separated the land and the land owner. Vast acres of farm land are owned or at least controlled by large multinational corporations which grow food in one nation, ship it to a second nation to be processed, and yet a third to actually be consumed. At the same time thousands of persons suffer from malnutrition in the nation where the food is actually produced.

We have also separated the stock market and the economy. The stock market no longer reflects the economic vitality of the world or of a particular nation. It now simply reflects the greed of a few investors and brokers. The dollar value of a stock does not reflect the worth of a corporation, its volume of business or any other indicator of a healthy economy. The value of the stock simply reflects a tight and closed circle of elite who circulate their money in a narrow, tightly knit circle which is disjointed from other segments of national and international life.

Ultimately we attempt to separate ourselves from our mistakes, even those of recent history. At the end of World War Two there were two defeated nations. Forty years after the war these two nations are among the more prosperous nations in the world. They both grew prosperous without the production and accumulation of weapons. The super powers of the world continued to pour more and more of their resources into weapons which continued to become increasingly more sophisticated and costly. As they did so, more and more social problems were created: hunger, poverty, drug abuse, alienation of people from each other. Yes! We are a disjointed society! Ultimately this alienation leads us to alienation from God. God is Life Itself, the fullest, most perfect, most complete expression of life. So as we become more disjointed from life around us we become increasingly disjointed from God." (1)

In 1963 I did my master's on the encyclical of Pope Leo XIII, <u>Rerum Novarum</u> (Of New Things) issued in 1891. At the time contemporary writings were advocating Socialism. Leo XIII spoke of political and economic philosophies which "separated labor from the person of the laborer and regarded it as a political and economic factor, as a commodity on the market of supply and demand." (2)

(1) Cf. Restoring the Common Wealth Chapter 8 a novel by William Crumley available through CreateSpace and Amazon

(2) Rerum Novarum Pope Leo XIII May 1891 sec. 131

In 1891 contemporary writing advocated Socialism, no private ownership. Leo spoke out strongly against such philosophy: "The Socialists, therefore, in endeavoring to transfer the possessions of individuals to the community strike out at the very interests of every wage earner, for they deprive him of the liberty of disposing of his wages, and thus of all possibility of increasing his stock and of bettering his condition in life." (3) In 1891 Leo XIII would not have known of the dangers of inflation. Today working people are deprived of the ability to dispose of their wages through continuing inflation.

In the last 50-60 years we have witnessed an increasing number of independent nations that collapsed. Jeffrey Sachs lists nearly 25 nations that have collapsed economically. He maintains that as a result of that economic collapse the USA needed to send in the U.S. military to help correct the problems caused by the collapse of the economy.(4) I raise a different question. Which caused which? Did the U.S or U.N. military go in to the countries to clean up bad economies or was there a U. S. presence there which helped to bring about the collapsed economy? Another way of asking that question: do collapsed economies bring on war? Or does war cause economies to collapse?

In another book <u>Why We Are Always Broke: things we need to know about the economy</u> I maintain that war is profitable. War also has drained the U.S. and other economies. That economic draining has been the cause of much of our debt (5). I did not begin researching the material in the book to reach that conclusion. A friend once said: "If you want to know why something happens, follow the money trail." I could see some truth to the statement. Still his statement seemed too simplistic. I began my research to prove him wrong. The more I researched, the broader I found the money trail is. (6)

(3) <u>Ibid</u>. secs 4-5

(4) Jeffrey D. Sachs <u>The End of Poverty: Economic Possibilities for Our Time</u> The Penguin Press New York 2005

(5) <u>Op. Cit</u>.

(6) <u>Ibid</u>.

Leo XIII continues: "In a preliminary and general way, it can be argued that the Western models to which African countries were aspiring were those projected to them by their former colonial masters, notably Britain, France, Portugal, and Spain. These countries have had the opportunities to impact on African institutions and ideas during the period of colonial subjugation when they attempted to integrate the economies of different African societies into the global capitalist economy they stemmed from. <u>Those years of colonial rule witnessed growth but not development in the economies of these colonial territories. In some instances, this growth was the product of introduced crops such as cocoa, coffee, tea, oil palm, cotton, sisal, and rubber, which the peasants were encouraged to add to their repertoire of crops or which European settlers or colonial commercial agencies cultivated as plantation crops.</u>" (7).

He goes on to say: "many Third World countries today, as well as much of world's economic history, is a function of institutional frameworks that overwhelmingly favor activities that promote redistributive rather than productive activity, that create monopolies rather than competitive conditions, and that restrict opportunities rather than expand them... . The organizations that develop in this institutional framework will become more efficient—but more efficient at making the society even more unproductive and the basic institutional structure even less conducive to productive activity" (8)

Leo XIII states that ownership of the land is an inherent natural right. "The right to possess private property is from nature, not from man; and the State has only the right to regulate its use in the interests of the public good, but by no means the right to abolish it altogether." (9) Henry George in an "open letter to Leo XIII states: "Clearly, the private ownership of land is from the state, not from nature" (10) George proposes to eliminate private property.

(6) <u>Ibid</u>.   (7) <u>Ibid</u>. emphasis added   (8 Leo XIII <u>Rerum Novarum</u> sec 35

(9) <u>Ibid</u>.   (10) cf. L.C.Knowles <u>Economic Development in the Nineteenth Century</u> (London, 1932)

Leo XIII apparently did not foresee the role of inflation in depriving the worker of the just benefits of his labor. Likewise, he does not mention ways in which the State has deprived individuals of their land. There are numerous examples of European nations going into what we now call "Third World Nations" and taking over the land in some cases, simply taking over the resources of the land in other cases. In the case of our own nation after the American Revolution and other wars the U.S. Government paid off its soldiers in land, the same land the U.S. Government had taken from the Natives. The U.S. Government also sells oil rights, gas rights and other privileges to huge corporations. These privileges allow them to extract the resources from this area as if they owned them.

In my thesis mentioned at the beginning of this section I quoted from L. C. Knowles. He points out that European workers were enticed to leave their homeland and settle in a foreign culture and environment and work for low wages. (11) Sachs seems to view it as an improvement but they stay in their own land and work for lower wages. Also we import laborers into our nation to leave their own homeland and work for low wages. Somehow we manage to convince ourselves that we are making progress. More significantly we convince ourselves that the persons whose labor we absorb are making progress. In the same book Knowles talks about the rise of trusts which destroy free competition that should exist in a healthy industry. He also points out that these trusts leave the worker even more at the mercy of capital.

Rerum Novarum rejected Socialism. In our day in capitalistic nations the most notorious Socialist state was Russia (The Union Of Soviet Socialist Republics). Actually the State owned nothing in the U.S.S.R. Everything (including the State) was owned by the Communist Party. In order to vote or hold office you had to be a member of the Communist Party. The Communist Party was simply Exxon and all the multi-national corporations rolled into one.

(11) cf. L.C.Knowles Economic Development in the Nineteenth Century (London, 1932)

More significant than Leo XIII's rejection of Socialism was his statement regarding what he believed to be the ultimate goal of a society that favored ownership over Capitalism: "The law, therefore, should favor ownership, and its policy should be to induce as many as possible to become owners." (12)

It is interesting what happened when the U.S.S.R. was dissolved. Estonia quickly ruled that no one (including the state) owned the land, the water or any of the natural elements. They belong to the people. In 2010 Bolivia passed similar legislation. It is too soon to see how this turn of events will play out.

Jeffrey Sachs (Cf. note 3 and accompanying text) mentions that extreme wealth only came in the last two centuries. (13) What he does not mention is that this accompanied the introduction of credit and debt. Credit was given to the purchaser but the State assumed the debt. Sachs does not mention that in the contemporary expression of this scenario banks do not give any real money or other asset. They simply extend a "line of credit" to the consumer. The state in turn issues a "Federal Reserve Note" which is a debt owed by the Federal Government to the Federal Reserve Bank, a coalition of privately owned banks. The only means of obtaining money available to the Federal Government is taxation.

Mr. Sachs heads up the United Nations Millennium Project and the Earth Institute at Columbia University. By his own admission the United Nations Millennium Project has "depended utterly on the Earth Institute." He lauds the scientific progress which has given us the tools to address modern problems of poverty. What he fails to acknowledge is that poverty was not created because we lacked proper scientific tools.

(12) Rerum Novarum sec 35

(13) Cf. Jeffrey D. Sachs <u>The End of Poverty: Economic Possibilities for Our Time</u> The Penguin Press New York 2005 pp 26-27

Poverty was created through greed and selfishness. Nowhere in his book do I find a reference to the Federal Reserve Bank or the Bank for International Settlements (BIS). Mr. Sachs worked for the World Bank. Surely he would be aware of these two major banks. (14)

Mr. Sachs tells about speaking to a group in India. In his talk he (to use his own words) was "waxing rhapsodic about the growth opportunities afforded by foreign direct investment." The group was not responding. He finally realized the British East India Company had done that centuries ago and turned India into a nation that was no longer economically independent. Mr. Sachs goes on to acknowledge that India had advantages in textile and clothing production when the British took over. It was the British military and British commerce which allowed the British to take over India. (15) In another part of the book he speaks very eloquently about women in Bangladesh making garments for sale in the USA. He does not seem to recognize that this is a contemporary expression of the British East Company in which a foreign corporation takes a lot more money out of a country than it puts into the country. If the women were being primed to form their own corporation and personally profit from their own labor and their own creativity it would be progress. When their labor is used to benefit a corporation in another nation it is simply a contemporary British East India Company.

Mr. Sachs seems to recognize the relationship of economic failure and military presence. He states that if the USA, Europe, Japan and other high income nations want to spend less time dealing with failed states then they have to spend more time dealing with failed economies. He then goes on to list 23 different nations in which the USA has had to intervene militarily because of the economic collapse of the nations. (16)

(14) Ibid. p. 224   (15) Ibid. pp. 171-173   (16) Ibid. pp. 332-334

Certainly his remarks could possibly be interpreted as meaning the USA and other high income nations need to revise their policy of protecting, at times even becoming advocates for major industries. The implication of his writing seemed to be the states failed due to their own policies rather than the U.S. and other high income nations' military and commerce taking over these nations in the same way the British East India Company did a few centuries earlier.

One thing some biographies of Jeffrey Sachs highlight is he advised Pope John Paul II on his encyclical Centesimus Annus. There are certain areas in which the Pope's encyclical differs from what Mr. Sachs seems to propose. One obvious difference is the Pope's encyclical is more in tune with the spiritual nature of human beings. That is to be expected. Pope John Paul II also concentrates on the writings of Pope Leo XIII. That also is to be expected. There are certain other differences in the writing of Jeffrey Sachs and Pope John Paul II. The Pope says: "While it is true that since 1945 weapons have been silent on the European continent, it must be remembered that true peace is never simply the result of military victory, but rather implies both the removal of the causes of war and genuine reconciliation between peoples. For many years there has been in Europe and the world a situation of non-war rather than genuine peace." (17)

Nowhere did I see Mr. Sachs speak about the role of genuine reconciliation between peoples. His emphasis seems simply to be economic and scientific. In the same section the Pope says: "An insane arms race swallowed up the resources needed for the development of national economies and for assistance to the less developed nations. Scientific and technological progress, which should have contributed to man's well-being, was transformed into an instrument of war: Science and technology were directed to the production of ever more efficient and destructive weapons." The Pope places part of the burden for poverty on science. Science and technology used its resources to produce ever more efficient destructive weapons. (18)

(17) Pope John Paul II Op. Cit. sec 18   (18) Ibid.

The Pope ends this section with an even clearer statement: "In addition, the precariousness of the peace which followed the Second World War was one of the principal causes of the militarization of many Third World countries and the fratricidal conflicts which afflicted them, as well as of the spread of terrorism and of increasingly barbaric means of political and military conflict. Moreover, the whole world was oppressed by the threat of an atomic war capable of leading to the extinction of humanity. Science used for military purposes had placed this decisive instrument at the disposal of hatred, strengthened by ideology. But if war can end without winners or losers in a suicide of humanity, then we must repudiate the logic which leads to it: the idea that the effort to destroy the enemy, confrontation and war itself are factors of progress and historical advancement. When the need for this repudiation is understood, the concepts of "total war" and "class struggle" must necessarily be called into question." (19)

"In general, such attempts endeavor to preserve free market mechanisms, ensuring, by means of a stable currency and the harmony of social relations, the conditions for steady and healthy economic growth in which people through their own work can build a better future for themselves and their families.

Then there are the other social forces and ideological movements which oppose Marxism by setting up systems of "national security", aimed at controlling the whole of society in a systematic way, in order to make Marxist infiltration impossible. By emphasizing and increasing the power of the State, they wish to protect their people from Communism, but in doing so they run the grave risk of destroying the freedom and values of the person, the very things for whose sake it is necessary to oppose Communism.

(19) Ibid.

Another kind of response, practical in nature, is represented by the affluent society or the consumer society. It seeks to defeat Marxism on the level of pure materialism by showing how a free-market society can achieve a greater satisfaction of material human needs than Communism, while equally excluding spiritual values. In reality, while on the one hand it is true that this social model shows the failure of Marxism to contribute to a humane and better society, on the other hand, insofar as it denies an autonomous existence and value to morality, law, culture and religion, it agrees with Marxism, in the sense that it totally reduces man to the sphere of economics and the satisfaction of material needs." (20)

"Decisive sectors of the economy still remain de facto in the hands of large foreign companies which are unwilling to commit themselves to the long-term development of the host country." (21)

The Pope warns that continuing this direction will ultimately affect the richer nations. "Europe cannot live in peace if the various conflicts which have arisen as a result of the past are to become more acute because of a situation of economic disorder, spiritual dissatisfaction and desperation." (22)

Pope John Paul II touches on the underlying causes of poverty, greed and selfishness in a later section of the encyclical. In the Pope's analysis this ultimately will have negative financial as well as moral consequences. "But profitability is not the only indicator of a firm's condition. It is possible for the financial accounts to be in order, and yet for the people — who make up the firm's most valuable asset — to be humiliated and their dignity offended. Besides being morally inadmissible, this will eventually have negative repercussions on the firm's economic efficiency.

(20) This entire quote is taken from Pope John Paul II Centisimus Annus sec. 19   (21) Ibid. sec 20   (22) Ibid. sec 28

In fact, the purpose of a business firm is not simply to make a profit, but is to be found in its very existence as a community of persons who in various ways are endeavoring to satisfy their basic needs, and who form a particular group at the service of the whole of society. Profit is a regulator of the life of a business, but it is not the only one; other human and moral factors must also be considered which, in the long term, are at least equally important for the life of a business.

At present, the positive efforts which have been made along these lines are being affected by the still largely unsolved problem of the foreign debt of the poorer countries. The principle that debts must be paid is certainly just. However, it is not right to demand or expect payment when the effect would be the imposition of political choices leading to hunger and despair for entire peoples. It cannot be expected that the debts which have been contracted should be paid at the price of unbearable sacrifices. In such cases it is necessary to find — as in fact is partly happening — ways to lighten, defer or even cancel the debt, compatible with the fundamental right of peoples to subsistence and progress". (23)

Section 41 of the encyclical contains one of the strongest statements of the Pope. It contains not simply a condemnation of Marxism and Socialism but a plea for a more just economic system. "The historical experience of the West, for its part, shows that even if the Marxist analysis and its foundation of alienation are false, nevertheless alienation — and the loss of the authentic meaning of life — is a reality in Western societies too. This happens in consumerism, when people are ensnared in a web of false and superficial gratifications rather than being helped to experience their personhood in an authentic and concrete way.

---

(23) Ibid. sec. 35

Alienation is found also in work, when it is organized so as to ensure maximum returns and profits with no concern whether the worker, through his own labour, grows or diminishes as a person, either through increased sharing in a genuinely supportive community or through increased isolation in a maze of relationships marked by destructive competitiveness and estrangement, in which he is considered only a means and not an end." (24)

In this context Pope John Paul II addresses another major problem, the media. "Exploitation, at least in the forms analyzed and described by Karl Marx, has been overcome in Western society. Alienation, however, has not been overcome as it exists in various forms of exploitation, when people use one another, and when they seek an ever more refined satisfaction of their individual and secondary needs, while ignoring the principal and authentic needs which ought to regulate the manner of satisfying the other ones too. A person who is concerned solely or primarily with possessing and enjoying, who is no longer able to control his instincts and passions, or to subordinate them by obedience to the truth, cannot be free: obedience to the truth about God and man is the first condition of freedom, making it possible for a person to order his needs and desires and to choose the means of satisfying them according to a correct scale of values, so that the ownership of things may become an occasion of growth for him. **This growth can be hindered as a result of manipulation by the means of mass communication, which impose fashions and trends of opinion through carefully orchestrated repetition, without it being possible to subject to critical scrutiny the premises on which these fashions and trends are based."** (25)

(24) <u>Ibid</u>. sec 41 emphasis mine

(25) <u>Ibid</u>. emphasis mine

The Pope's analysis of the economic factors which are distorting human nature is very accurate. However he seems to blame socialistic nations and philosophies for these errors. He states that Western society has "overcome" exploitation. The problem in the West is not economic but consumerism which is stirred on by the media. He is correct in that analysis. However, he seems to diminish the economic forces which drive consumerism and the media. For me, Jeffrey Sachs who advised him on the encyclical seems to take this same approach.

The latter part of Pope John Paul II's encyclical seems to show the clearest indication of the effect of Jeffrey Sachs' influence in the writing of Pope John Paul II. "Ownership of the means of production, whether in industry or agriculture, is just and legitimate if it serves useful work. It becomes illegitimate, however, when it is not utilized or when it serves to impede the work of others, in an effort to gain a profit which is not the result of the overall expansion of work and the wealth of society, but rather is the result of curbing them or of illicit exploitation, speculation or the breaking of solidarity among working people. Ownership of this kind has no justification, and represents an abuse in the sight of God and man.

The obligation to earn one's bread by the sweat of one's brow also presumes the right to do so. A society in which this right is systematically denied, in which economic policies do not allow workers to reach satisfactory levels of employment, cannot be justified from an ethical point of view, nor can that society attain social peace. Just as the person fully realizes himself in the free gift of self, so too ownership morally justifies itself in the creation, at the proper time and in the proper way, of opportunities for work and human growth for all" (26)

Nowhere in the encyclical does the Pope seem to recognize the problem of the creation of debt by banks as an integral part of the process of owning the means of production. Section 48 could be a veiled reference to the problem of banks using debt to create more wealth

---

(26) Ibid. sec 24

"The absence of stability, together with the corruption of public officials and the spread of improper sources of growing rich and of easy profits deriving from illegal or purely speculative activities, constitutes one of the chief obstacles to development and to the economic order." (27) (This could be a veiled reference to making money thru debt but the section also refers to drugs and other illegal activity.)

"The individual today is often suffocated between two poles represented by the State and the marketplace. At times it seems as though he exists only as a producer and consumer of goods, or as an object of State administration. People lose sight of the fact that life in society has neither the market nor the State as its final purpose, since life itself has a unique value which the State and the market must serve. Man remains above all a being who seeks the truth and strives to live in that truth, deepening his understanding of it through a dialogue which involves past and future generations." (28)

The Pope presents the State and the marketplace as two opposing poles. This seems to show little sense that the marketplace has a dominant influence on the State. In fact, the State at times even acts as the agent of the marketplace. This is the same philosophy Jeffrey Sachs seems to advocate.

In section 52 the Pope states: "Furthermore, it must not be forgotten that at the root of war there are usually real and serious grievances: injustices suffered, legitimate aspirations frustrated, poverty, and the exploitation of multitudes of desperate people who see no real possibility of improving their lot by peaceful means.

(27) Ibid. sec. 48

(28) Ibid. sec 49

For this reason, another name for peace is development. (sec. 105) Just as there is a collective responsibility for avoiding war, so too there is a collective responsibility for promoting development. Just as within individual societies it is possible and right to organize a solid economy which will direct the functioning of the market to the common good, so too there is a similar need for adequate interventions on the international level. For this to happen, a great effort must be made to enhance mutual understanding and knowledge, and to increase the sensitivity of consciences. This is the culture which is hoped for, one which fosters trust in the human potential of the poor, and consequently in their ability to improve their condition through work or to make a positive contribution to economic prosperity. But to accomplish this, the poor — be they individuals or nations — need to be provided with realistic opportunities. Creating such conditions demands a concerted worldwide effort to promote development. It demands an effort which also involves sacrificing the positions of income and of power enjoyed by the more developed economies. (sec.106)

This may mean making important changes in established life-styles, in order to limit the waste of environmental and human resources, thus enabling every individual and all the peoples of the earth to have a sufficient share of those resources. In addition, the new material and spiritual resources must be utilized which are the result of the work and culture of peoples who today are on the margins of the international community, so as to obtain an overall human enrichment of the family of nations." (29)

This is one of the clearest calls for change but still there is no direct reference to the false creation of "wealth" through debt. No sense that what we term "wealth" often has no basis in anything real. No effective change will occur until this problem is addressed.

(29) Ibid. Sec. 52

CONCLUSION

Somehow the evils addressed by Leo XIII still exist 122 years later. Marvelous advances have taken place in science and technology but we still have poverty. Cell phones and the internet allow us to communicate with persons almost anywhere in the world. A disproportionate number of people do not know the names of their neighbors. The needs of people are often subordinate to profit. The media enhances, promotes, it might even be said advocates, violence. We will not solve any of these problems by using the same approach. They will not be solved by throwing more money at the problem. At one time money represented a similar amount of human labor and human creativity. Today, a disproportionate amount of money simply represents a corresponding debt.

As in 1891 the laborer is still a commodity on the economic market. Laborers are told if you are not willing to take pay cuts or receive fewer benefits we will hire someone who is willing to take a lesser pay. The difference between highest paid employees and lowest paid employees continues to expand. We too often are willing to equate growth with development. So often we limit growth to economic growth. The Dow Jones average has grown sharply. So has the number of persons living below the poverty level. Growth does not mean development. Two years ago we saw something I never would have imagined – citizens occupying banks and financial institutions.

In 1891 Pope Leo XIII lamented the fact that the laborer had become a commodity of the marketplace. At least labor is a positive force. It produces something that is of service to mankind. Modern bankers and economists have discovered how to make debt a commodity of the marketplace. Corporations can borrow millions (sometimes even billions) of dollars. In turn the same corporations can take that debt and borrow a similar amount of money on their debt.

Chapter 5 Economic aspects of war

When we look at the cost of war there are many factors to consider: money spent, lives lost, families disrupted, what those lives could have produced if they had not been wasted in war. Some of these costs are not easy to assess. Most of the costs are disputed. Governments give us one assessment. Groups less favorable to war usually give us a higher assessment of the cost. We will attempt to look at some of the costs.

COSTS OF WORLD WAR ONE

Allied Powers	Cost in Dollars in 1914
United States	22,625,253,000
Great Britain	35,334,012,000
France	24,265,583,000
Russia	22,293,950,000
Italy	12,413,998,000
Belgium	1,154,468,000
Romania	1,600,000,000
Japan	40,000,000
Serbia	399,400,000
Greece	270,000,000
Canada	1,665,576,000
Australia	1,423,208,000
New Zealand	378,750,000
India	601,279,000
South Africa	300,000,000
British Colonies	125,000,000
Others	500,000,000
Total of all Costs	**125,690,477,000**
Central Powers	Cost in Dollars in 1914-18
Germany	37,775,000,000
Austria-Hungary	20,622,960,000
Turkey	1,430,000,000
Bulgaria	815,200,000
Total of all Costs	**60,643,160,000**
TOTAL COST	**$186,333,637,000 (1)**

The estimated population of the United States in 1914 was 99,111,000 persons. The average cost per person was $228.28. A family of four would spend $913 on the war.

(1) Cf. Spartacus Educational Financial costs of World War 1 http://www.spartacus.schoolnet.co.uk/FWWcosts.htm

The cost for World War Two was significantly higher as the following indicates: "The total cost of WW2 was upwards of $1.6 trillion though many financial records for 1939 are missing, incomplete, misleading or contradictory. Country's spending was as follows; USA $350 billion, UK $150 billion, France $100 billion, USSR $200 billion, Germany $300 billion, Italy $50 billion, Japan $100 billion and all other participants $350 billion." (2)

The population of the USA in 1945 was about 140 million persons. $350 billion would equal $2500 per person or $10,000 for a family of four. The cost of the wars in Korea and Vietnam were just over a trillion dollars. The cost of war is escalating. The U. S. says wars in Iraq and Afghanistan cost the U.S. A. roughly $1.5 trillion. This was the amount of money officially allocated by the U.S. Congress. (3) The figures include money allocated through fiscal year (FY) 2010. Money has continued to be spent since FY 2010. The figure $1.5 trillion was reached by dividing the total amount allocated 2003-2010 by 8 and multiplying that figure by 11 to account for the additional three years expenditure. In fact the allocation amount has risen steadily after the end of the war.

Non-governmental agencies project the costs of the Iraq and Afghanistan war much higher than government estimates. The "Costs of War" project of the Watson Institute at Brown University cites the cost at four trillion dollars. It states that over 330,000 people died due to direct war violence, many more indirectly. It estimates that there are 7.4 million refugees because of the war. Despite the promise of a better life for the residents of Iraq the country remains war devastated after U.S. withdrawal from Iraq. The report mentions that the four trillion dollar cost does not include the interest cost on the money which had to be borrowed to pay for the war. (4)

(2) cf. http://www.ask.com/question/how-much-did-world-war-2-cost

(3) This data from "Financial Costs of the Iraq War" in Wikipedia. It does not include allocations for the war in Afghanistan. Cf. http://en.wikipedia.org/wiki/Financial_cost_of_the_Iraq_War

(4) Op. cit. cf http://costsofwar.org

What the Watson Institute and other studies do not point out is the cause of the war in Iraq. It was presented as a response to the bombings of September 11, 2001 and Sadaam Hussein building nuclear weapons. A United Nations investigation found no nuclear weapons being constructed in Iraq. We were not told that Sadaam Hussein was in the process of investing Iraqi money in Euros and taking the money out of U.S. dollars. One of the first actions of the USA in seizing control of Iraq was to place all Iraq money under control of the U.S. Federal Reserve Bank. This money was to be placed in the Bank for International Settlements in Basle, Switzerland (5)

The Bank for International Settlements was set up after World War One. Its stated purpose was to pay off the German and British debt from World War One. Why almost 100 years later does the Bank still exist? There are several reasons it should have ceased to exist. 1) The purpose of its existence is gone, the debt has been paid. 2) The agency which set it up (the League of Nations) no longer exists and the court it created ceased to exist when the League was dissolved. Why did the Bank not also cease to exist? 3) In July 1944 a conference was held at Bretton Woods, New Hampshire. This conference set up the World Bank and other banking institutions to ensure a peaceful solution to world events after World War Two ended. One of its recommendations was to shut down the Bank for International Settlements. The Bank still exists.

When I researched <u>Why We Are Always Broke</u> I visited the Bretton Woods, New Hampshire site of the conference which set up the World Bank. One of the guides was very interested in my research. He gave me a special tour. He was a high school student and had worked in the kitchen during the conference. His girlfriend worked as a waitress serving meals to the delegates. They married and still lived together at the time I visited there. He described cars with "United Nations" symbols which regularly carried people to and from the conference.

(5) <u>Cf</u>. <u>Why We Are Always Broke</u> Chapter 8 p, 135

I questioned the guide about a "United Nations" vehicle transporting people to and from the conference. I remembered the "United Nations" being set up AFTER the end of World War Two. How could "United Nations" vehicles be in New Hampshire in 1944 when the "United Nations" did not even exist? He was adamant that the vehicles bore a United Nations sign. In my research I found that the United Nations had been set up January 1, 1942 less than a month after the Japanese attack on Pearl Harbor. On that date 26 nations signed a pact to overthrow the Axis Powers. So, in its origins the United Nations was a military organization not a "peace keeping" group as its current propaganda suggests. The guide also maintained that the "United Nations" was in charge of the conference. It was not simply transporting people to and from the conference.

About a year after the United Nations was set up the United Nations Relief and Rehabilitation Administration (UNRRA) was set up. Its function was to rehabilitate European nations economically devastated by World War Two. In its origins the United Nations was military and economic. The two functions were united. I described this connection in the following quote from Chapter 5 of <u>Why We Are Always Broke</u>.

"Few persons realize that this is the underlying rationale behind the United Nations. Even fewer seem to take enough time to reflect that wars are very profitable for those who manufacture weapons, uniforms, flags as well as for those who negotiate peace, for medics, those who supply medicines and other medical supplies and services. Wars are also very profitable for those who come in to clean up and rebuild after the war is over. The forces which set up the United Nations were very much aware of the central role that war plays in economics as well as the central role economics plays in wars. So did the forces which were responsible for the setting up of the Central Intelligence Agency." (6)

(6) <u>Op. Cit</u>. Chapter 5 page 80

The Central Intelligence Agency was set up in the administration of President Harry Truman. I was able to find information regarding the origins of that Agency in the Truman Presidential Library in Independence, Missouri. The Agency was set up with economic goals rather than military goals as we are often led to believe.

"Thus the greatest present danger to U.S. security lies, not in the military strength of the U.S.S.R. and the possibility of Soviet armed aggression, <u>but in the possibility of the economic collapse of Western Europe and of the consequent accession to power of elements subservient to the Kremlin</u>. The economic weakness of Western Europe is the result of the simultaneous impact of extensive physical destruction, a breakdown in pre-war economic sources. ... a deterioration in the will and capacity to work and in other driving forces of a virile economy, and a probably irreparable loss of large pre-war claims for goods and services derived from overseas investments and from a dominant position in colonial territories." (7)

The report goes on to detail what each nation must do to prevent this economic collapse which will lead to the Kremlin's "accession to power". It is difficult to read this document without recognizing that the fear of those who gave initial force to the CIA was not the fear of a superior economic force overcoming our own. What they feared most was that our own western economic system was about to collapse.

The report looks at each European nation and highlights what our response needs to be. Each response is economic. Nowhere in the report is freedom or democracy mentioned. The entire focus is on economic factors. The first nation highlighted is Great Britain.

(7) Central Intelligence Agency: <u>Review of the World Situation as it Relates to the Security of the United States</u>: 26 September, 1947, declassified April, 1977 Harry S. Truman Library, Independence Mo. (emphasis added)

The report states that Britain "must curtail drastically its overseas commitments, with a consequent reduction of power and influence abroad. Existing British overseas commitments are so extensive and important that their precipitate liquidation would create conditions prejudicial to security interests of the United States." (8)

The report looks at the economic crisis about to erupt in France. The report mentions that the Communist Party is already the strongest single party in France and an economic collapse might bring them to power. The report looks at the economic distress in Germany and in Italy. It mentions the proximity of Yugoslavia to Italy and Tito assuming power in Yugoslavia may influence Italy. Nowhere does the report talk about the failure of political systems. In every case the fear lies in the collapse of the economic system.

One of the greatest fears is the collapse of Greece. Communist forces have taken over partial control of the Greek Government. "The Greek Government is unable to cope with this threat without active aid. At any time U.S. armed intervention may be required to prevent its collapse ... The loss of Greece would not only impair the strategic position in the Eastern Mediterranean, but would also have profound psychological repercussions throughout Western Europe and the Near and the Middle East." (9)

Greece was the first nation to which we sent troops to subdue the communists. Greece is still in economic disorder almost seventy years after the establishment of the CIA. The review cites the Near East as important because of its proximity to vast amounts of oil. Because of this importance we must keep friendly relations with the Nation of Israel. But much oil is in Arab nations. So we have to balance Israeli support with support of Arab nations.

(8) Ibid.   (9) Ibid.

The review states the Israelis are exploiting the Nazi persecution of Jews to gain world-wide sympathy for their cause. They are doing so to the disadvantage of the Arabs who now identify the United States and the United Kingdom as solidly pro- Israel. This could be a problem if they decide to turn over the operation of their oil interests to the Soviet Union. We need to keep the Arabs happy also.   (10)

Original CIA documents indicate the CIA was set up because of a fear of the economic collapse of Europe. That collapse was due to extensive colonization by European nations. Somehow the persons who wrote the initial CIA documents did not see that the USA taking over the control of the British and French empires would lead us to the same end. This is summarized in a quote from Why We Always Broke.

"From the earliest documents of the CIA it is clear economics is the underlying force which will determine CIA activity and policy. It also molds the political and military direction they will attempt to lead the United States. It is the same direction they will attempt to drive other nations. One of the underlying themes is the U.S.A. must take over funding and controlling the former British Empire. What no one initially seemed to understand was that Britain and France lost their empires through economic forces not military forces. We will have the same fate when we try to take on their economic responsibilities."   (11)

There was also a more balanced focus in CIA material. It is found in material in the Truman Library under the "Rose Conway File". The report begins with a statement that there is no mechanism for evaluating the role of U.S. Industry in our war effort. The propaganda of industry leads us to believe they have given their all and have made enormous contributions to our safety. A critical review "will reveal great sectors of the most dismal and regrettable failure."   (12)

(10) cf. Ibid.   (11) Cf. Why We Are Always Broke chapter 5 p. 82

(12) Harry Truman Library, Rose Conway Files, Technical Series Report No. 51 May 31, 1945 p. 1

The report cites the more serious problems in the attitude and work of industry:

1. Industry has used universities to glean workers for their industry rather than promote research.
2. The work done was paid for by government. The results should belong to government rather than accrue to the private coffers of the corporations.
3. Claims that the material falls under "security" shields prevents the Congress from being able to freely examine the material and the evidence.
4. The government needs to give direction and impetus to scientific research not industry which is motivated by financial gain rather than the good of the Nation. (13)

In addition to the role of the United Nations and the Central Intelligence Agency we need to look at another phenomenon which has evolved since the end of World War. Virtually every nation now has a central bank. These central banks control the flow of money in the various nations. They also facilitate the flow of money between nations. The banks operate for the benefit of international bankers rather than the individual member nations.

Central banking can be traced to medieval public banks. In Barcelona the Taula de Canvi (Municipal Bank of Deposit) was established in 1401 for the safekeeping of city and private deposits, but it was also expected to help fund Barcelona's government (particularly the financing of military expenses), which it did by receiving tax payments and issuing bonds ... During the 1460s, however, excessive demands for lending ... led to its liquidation and reorganization. (14)

(13) Harry Truman Library Rose Conway Files: "Technical Series Report No. 51 May 31, 1945 pp. 2-4

(14) http://www.britannica.com/EBchecked/topic/51892/bank/273051/The-origins-of-central-banking
(emphasis added)

During the 17th and 18th centuries the Amsterdamsche Wisselbank was founded. The bank's conservative lending policy allowed it to maintain reserves that fully covered its outstanding notes and thereby rendered it invulnerable even to the major panic provoked by Louis XIV's unexpected invasion of the Netherlands in 1672. Eventually its reserves shrank and its reputation suffered after it granted large-scale loans to the Dutch East India Company and the Dutch government. (15)

"The Bank of England, founded in 1694 for the purpose of advancing £1.2 million to the British government to fund its war against France, eventually became the world's most powerful and influential financial institution. It was the first public bank to assume most of the characteristics of modern central banks, including acceptance, by the late 19th century, of an official role in preserving the integrity of England's banking and monetary system (as opposed to merely looking after its own profits). By 1800 the Bank of England had become the country's only limited-liability joint-stock bank, its charter having denied other banks the right to issue banknotes (then an essential source of bank funding). Its size and prestige encouraged deposits from other banks and thereby streamlined the process of interbank debt settlement and confirmed the Bank of England's status as the 'bankers' bank.'" (16)

"The history of the Bank was closely tied to war efforts of the British Empire. During World War One the National Debt jumped to seven billion pounds. The 'solution' was to abandon the gold standard in 1931. So, the Bank no longer was required to back its notes with gold. The abandonment of the gold standard was not the solution. So, after World War Two the Bank was nationalized. This did not work either. So, in 1998 control of the central bank was returned to private investors." (17)

---

(15) Ibid.
(16) Ibid.
(17) Cf. Why We Are Always Broke. Ch 3 pp. 41-42

BANCO de ESPANA (THE BANK OF SPAIN) is the central bank of Spain. It was founded in 1782 as a private bank under royal patronage. The bank's growth depended on the growth of the public debt. Like most central banks it had sole control over the issuing of currency. <u>The Bank fared well for a few years until a continuous series of wars from 1793 to 1814 led the Bank into serious difficulties</u>. One "solution" was to create several banks which were allowed to issue bank notes as currency. This system prevailed from 1829 until 1844. (18)

THE BANK OF FRANCE was created by Napoleon Bonaparte in 1800. A few years earlier the Government had backed the fiasco of John Law (19) and ended up with a large burden. For this reason the founders of the Bank of France believed the people would not trust a government owned bank. Napoleon and his group were the stockholders of the Bank. The Bank was to have a stock base worth thirty million Francs. The Bank opened in February 1803. It had exclusive rights to issue paper money in Paris. The Bank was different from other central banks. Its original charter limited its activity to Paris rather than all of France. And, the bank was not protected from competition of existing banks. (20)

BANQUE DE REPUBLIQUE D'HÔTE was an early "New World" central bank of Haiti. It was first established by a German group in 1825. The country had been devastated by a fifteen year war of independence. One of the main purposes of the bank was to help mobilize the natural resources of the country. The bank developed in the aftermath of a war. It was founded by foreign (European) interests and its purpose was to mobilize the natural resources of the nation. These resources were not used for the good of the people of Haiti. Early banks in Haiti were formed by German, French, and United States groups. (21)

---

(18) <u>Ibid</u>. p. 43 emphasis added

(19) John Law was the first modern person to use credit. He got the French Government to back a financial fiasco in the "New World". It was not backed by anything real but "notes" he put out. In exchange for these "notes" people gave time and labor, even went to a new land. When the venture failed, John Law got the French Government to pay for his loss.
(20) Cf. <u>Why We Are Always Broke</u>. Ch 3 p. 43   (21) <u>Ibid</u>. p. 45

NARODOWY BANK POLSKI (Polish National Bank) has an interesting history. Attempts to place the Bank in the hands of private bankers have failed. The Bank has maintained its primary object to protect the silver standard and safeguard the value of its silver. It has been a strong state owned bank to counterbalance privately owned banks. The Sveriques Riksbank has avoided the tendency of other European banks the last 60 years. The Bank was not nationalized after World War Two and did not join the European Union of Central Banks. Poland has been a frequent victim of war. With each defeat the central bank has come under the control of a different ruling group. (22)

The report in <u>Why We Are Always Broke</u> lists the various nations which have seized control of the Polish National Bank over the years. In 1989 Poland began to change to a "market" based economy as opposed to a state based economy. Commercial banks began to reappear in Poland. Unlike Western central banks, Narodowy Bank Polski did not issue large numbers of notes to "strengthen' the economy. It actually reduced the number of slotting (Polish currency) present in order to restore the purchasing power of the currency. A new slotting was issued. 10,000 old slots were redeemable for a single new slotting.

However, if you look at their website today it is clear that as hard as the bank has struggled to keep their currency from inflating they are subject to elements beyond their control: rising oil prices, rising labor prices, loss of value of the major currencies (dollar, pound, Euro e.g.). They seem to be in better shape than many economies but are still under stress because of the problems imposed on them by the "stronger" economies. (23)

(22) Ibid. pp. 43-45   (23(Ibid.

THE CENTRAL BANK OF THE REPUBLIC OF TURKEY was initially owned by the British. In 1856 when it was set up, it was called the "Ottoman Bank" and was financed by British and French capital. In 1863 it became a state bank under the name of "Imperial Ottoman Bank". This bank alone had the right to issue bank notes. It collected all state revenues. Interest and principal payments of all debts foreign and domestic would be made to the Ottoman Bank only. The Bank exercised all major functions of a contemporary central bank.

There were 135,000 shares of stock in the Bank. 80,000 were owned by a British group. 50,000 were owned by a French group. Only 5,000 were owned by Ottomans. Today the bank is known as the Central Bank of the Republic of Turkey. The Turkish Government owns about 55% of the Bank stock.   (24)

Two central banks were established in 1880, the National Bank of Romania and the Banco de la Republica of Colombia. The National Bank of Romania) is the central bank of Romania. <u>During World War One the German military seized the Bank's head office and all of its assets in Bucharest. The Bank treasury was moved to Jassy then later sent to Russia.</u> After the war it was moved back to Bucharest. In 1920 the Bank was given the right to issue currency. In 1925 the State once again became one of the stockholders of the Bank. <u>In 1945 the Communist regime seized power and took over the control of the Bank. The Bank remained under their control for forty five years.</u> Since 1990 the Bank has been attempting to restore itself to a previous base where it was part state owned and part privately owned.   (25) Seizure of the bank by the Communists in 1945 was one of the causes for fear of the Communists. It is the opinion of the author that a major fear of Communism was not a totalitarian government. We supported many such governments. A major fear was that someone other than the bankers would control the world.

(24) <u>Ibid.</u> p. 42   (25) <u>Ibid.</u> p. 46 emphasis added

BANCO de la REPUBLICA (COLOMBIA) BANK OF THE REPUBLIC was organized as an autonomous bank with an initial capital of ten million pesos. Half (50%) of the capital came from the Government. The rest came from foreign and national commercial banks as well as from private individuals. In September, 1931 England dismantled the gold standard which was linked to the value of their currency, the pound sterling. So, the Colombian Government temporarily suspended trading with gold and the conversion of currency into gold. Still the role of the Bank continued to expand. The Board of Directors began to expand. It added representatives from the National Federation of Coffee Producers, from the Chambers of Commerce, and ultimately from the unions to their board. In 1973 the Bank was nationalized. Although under direct supervision and control of the State, the Bank retained a significant degree of autonomy. The Bank was able to freely analyze monetary phenomena, design and apply monetary policy. They were free to do their primary job: safeguard the purchasing power of the national currency. Colombia is unique. The Government retained control over the bank. No other nation actually shut down a central bank because it failed to do its job.

The Bank has retained and utilized most powers of a central bank: 1. The Bank is the only one able to issue bank notes as legal tender. 2. The Bank cannot issue credit to private individuals and operates under very strict conditions in issuing bonds to Government. 3. It is a banker to banks. It stringently controls the amount of money in circulation. 4. It Regulates foreign and exchange market to protect and defend the exchange rate. 5. It Administers international reserves. 6. It is the Government's banker. (26)

---

(26) Ibid. p. 46

By 1880 less than twenty central banks had been created. Most of them were European based. They served two major functions. 1. They funded wars and military operations. 2. They provided the revenues for the economic exploitation of colonial nations by European powers. By the end of World War Two most early central banks (those created before 1900) had abandoned their original focus of issuing only enough currency that could be converted into available gold and/or silver. Central banks had begun to discount notes, to represent governments in business deals and to create an international monetary network.

Roughly 75% of the world's central banks have been founded since the end of World War Two. Roughly 25% of them have been founded since 1990. In the last thirty years there have been a series of international central banks formed which brings a whole new dimension to banking and international finance. In the last fifteen years we have seen the creation of central banks of central bankers, e.g. The Bank of Central African states, the European Union, Islamic Central bank.

The Islamic world is taking great steps to counter the action of modern central banks. For example, the Constitution of Egypt takes a very new approach to constitutions. Instead of emphasizing the Government and its socio-economic role, the first one third of the Constitution emphasizes the rights of Egyptian citizens and anyone who comes to Egypt. The second major focus of the first one third of the Egyptian Constitution is the freedoms granted to its citizens and the responsibility of the State to protect and foster these freedoms.

A second major effort of the Islamic World is a decision of the Supreme court of Pakistan. This decision renders it illegal to charge any interest in Pakistan. Only Great Britain and the United States of America seem totally committed to maintaining an economy based on interest and exploitation.

The Central Bank of Haiti developed in the aftermath of a war. It was founded by foreign (European) interests and its purpose was to mobilize the natural resources of the nation. These resources were not used for the good of the people of Haiti.

Central banks are closely linked to war. In wars governments acquire huge debts. Central banks issue notes which finance these debts. When these debts cannot be paid off gold reserves are drained from government treasuries. Governments then lose control of the banks. One of the few nations that have managed to keep control of its banks is Sweden. Sweden has been very free of wars and has not gone into debt. The Iran-Contra Affair unveiled the work of private arms dealers in selling arms illegally. Manucher Ghorbanifar and Adnan Khashoggi were two of the more notorious persons involved in the sale of arms. An analysis of the war with Iraq in this century also has revealed corruption in wars and the sale of arms and military services. Recent wars have revealed that a significant amount of military activity is now performed by private (non-governmental) groups. The conclusion of the book <u>Why We Are Always Broke</u> states it this way: "**We attempted to create free elections and help Iraqi people become politically independent. But no attempt has been made to help the Iraqi people become economically independent. In fact their central bank is under the control of the Federal Reserve System of the United States. Their funds are deposited in the Bank for International Settlements in Switzerland. Their elected officials have no oversight powers over their central bank. We react strongly to terrorism but promote economic terrorism.**

The companies set up to do business in Iraq are predominantly British and/or American. Most of them are paramilitary. Much of the civil unrest in Iraq is a reaction to these military forces imposed on the Iraqi people. In addition to terrorizing the people they are also economically exploiting them. Iraqi workers are paid only enough to buy a small amount of meat. Foreign mercenaries doing the same work are paid considerably more. Foreigners performing oversight services receive $400 to $1000 a day.

"Security" companies are now a major force in our nation and in the world. They are all private corporations and so no one has oversight of them. One company may in turn own twenty or more other "security" companies. The "security" companies that are "protecting" us in Iraq are the same people who set Saddam Hussein in power and promoted Osama bin Laden.

We do not realize that many of the conditions imposed on the Iraqi people are also being imposed on us. Neither we as individuals nor our elected officials have any control over our money. The Federal Reserve Bank which controls our money (and now the Iraqi money) is a group of private bankers. It is they who create the money. Each dollar created is a dollar of debt owed by our government to this private group of bankers. Sadaam Hussein was killed not because of human treachery and the killing of many people. Sadaam Hussein was a threat and therefore killed because he took Iraqi money and placed it in Euros, the official currency of the European Central Bank.

Great Britain and the USA are two nations who have the most to lose if the European Central Bank succeeds. They are the two nations who most pushed the war in Iraq. "Homeland Security" is the brain child of the man who initially oversaw the Coalition Provisional Authority in Iraq. In the days after Hurricane Katrina that act was used to bring in the same forces that were terrorizing Iraqi people to terrorize people in New Orleans. President Bush tried to repeal the ban on using US troops in domestic law enforcement and allow security firms to install their paramilitaries on US soil. What we have done in Iraq is coming home to haunt us in yet another ominous way. (27)

(27) Cf. Why We Are Always Broke conclusion of chapter 8 p. 135

Is there an alternative to war? To put that question in the context of this book we need to ask: What could the money we spend on war be used for? President Eisenhower gave us a clue in one of his speeches. Some people question the numbers but no one can question the fact that many more essential human needs could be met if we did not spend our money on wars.

"Every gun that is made, every warship launched, every rocket fired signifies, in the final sense, a theft from those who hunger and are not fed, those who are cold and are not clothed. This world in arms is not spending money alone. It is spending the sweat of its laborers, the genius of its scientists, the hopes of its children.

The cost of one modern heavy bomber is this: a modern brick school in more than 30 cities. It is two electric power plants, each serving a town of 60,000 population. It is two fine, fully equipped hospitals. It is some 50 miles of concrete highway.

We pay for a single fighter plane with a half-million bushels of wheat. We pay for a single destroyer with new homes that could have housed more than 8,000 people.

This, I repeat, is the best way of life to be found on the road the world has been taking. This is not a way of life at all, in any true sense. Under the cloud of threatening war, it is humanity hanging from a cross of iron." (28)

---

(28) Dwight Eisenhower *Address by President Dwight D. Eisenhower "The Chance for Peace" delivered before the American Society of Newspaper Editors, April 16, 1953.*

An analysis of the speech says: "Unfortunately, there is no solid evidence as to how Mr. Hughes and Mr. Nitze came up with those figures. Historians at the Dwight D. Eisenhower Presidential Library in Abilene, Kan., could not determine how the numbers were assessed. But a quick spot check of one commodity does give some confidence that the quantities were not completely pulled out of a hat.

A look at an earlier draft of the speech shows that the "fighter jet" cited would buy 170,000 bushels of wheat, versus a half-million as stated in the final version. With wheat running about $2 a bushel then, a quick search of United States Air Force aircraft of the time shows that the earlier draft might have referred to the F-86 Sabre, which cost $211,111 at the time. However, the higher figure in the final draft might have referred to the new F-84F Thunderstreak, which cost $769,330.

Chapter 6 The perfect Nazi

Material in this book was previously presented in a novel, <u>Restoring the Common WEALTH</u>. One theme of the novel is that events we have been told are not related are really inter-related. In the novel I connect the CIA, the U.S. State Department, and the Nazi Central Bank. I join the Mafia and the CIA. I trace the connection between various corporations who profit from war and the sale of war materials.

Despite their being connected in their profit making efforts I recognize that they each have their own agenda which at times is opposed to that of other corporations. The novel also ties together drug dealing, Vatican Bank scandals, and U.S. Government scandals. I describe the role of international banks set up after World War One and World War Two. I mention that for every dollar invested in third world nations three dollars leaves that nation in favor of corporations in richer nations. I mention that this is actually stated in one of the reports of the large international banks.

One of the chapters in the novel is entitled <u>The perfect Nazi</u>. That chapter and some other chapters describe how the predecessor of the Central Intelligence Agency (CIA) was able to help Nazis escape from Europe after World War Two. Chapter five of this book looks at an early document of the CIA. That document describes the role envisioned by the CIA from its first days. They are to prevent the Communists from taking over the faltering economy of Europe which has been economically devastated by World War Two. The novel presents the CIA as the contemporary perfect Nazi.

Another chapter of the novel is entitled <u>Not another story</u>. That chapter looks at an alternative way of looking at the land and an alternative way of looking at who we are. I end this book with the material presented in that chapter.

Whitney had his own connections. He was a Native American. His ancestors had no written language. Their history was passed on by word of mouth, especially by music, poetry, and stories. Whitney was particularly impressed with Pope Victor's homily, especially his reference to the disjointed society.

After listening to the pope's mass Whitney called Eloise James. They met in the park. Whitney related one of his stories which described a very early contact between his people and European settlers. Whitney insisted that they were settlers.

"They had not come to see how we lived. They came to settle. They wanted the land. They were interested in making money off of the land. We had no idea what money was. We bartered for everything we needed. We didn't own anything. We could not even imagine anyone owning the land."

Whitney paused. He recalled David's remarks. "I understood David very well when he talked about the common wealth. Land, air, water, light are our common wealth. No one can own any of them. They exist for the benefit of everyone.

Whitney picked up a large stick, drew a big circle on the ground. "That was our land."

He drew a ring around part of that land. "That was where we lived. We lived together. In the colder months we built little tepees to shield ourselves from the cold."

He drew another ring. "That was where we produced the food we needed to eat." Through the middle of the area He drew a crooked line. "That was the river. It provided us with some of our food and other needs. We also needed to trade with neighboring groups. They also could share with us. The river allowed us to trade"

Most of the area was not within the living area and the garden area. "What happened to the rest of the area?" Eloise James asked.

"That land belonged to the other residents."

"Other residents?"

"Yes, the deer, the bear, the birds, the trees. All the other creatures."

"That's the majority of the land!"

"They are the majority of the population."

Whitney paused as he allowed these ideas to penetrate the being of Eloise James. Then he continued. "We believed that we all had to survive together. We needed the animals for food. The deer provided us with clothing. Their bones provided us with tools. The trees gave us some food, protection from the sun and with transportation. We needed to protect them for our own welfare.

Whitney erased the ring where the food was produced. He drew another ring in another area. "We could not just continue to use the same spot for growing our food. We had to let the area rest. So we moved our farming area to another place in our land. We were always careful to protect the trees in each area. They were our shade, some of our food, and they were necessary for the life of our fellow creatures."

It all seemed so simple, too simple for people who live in such a complicated world today. Eloise James wondered how it all broke down. Before she had a chance to express that Whitney erased all the lines in the circle.

Then he said: "There is another way of looking at the land. That way also affects the way we look at ourselves." Whitney began drawing small squares throughout the entire area of the land. "The Europeans began to teach my ancestors that individuals could own the land. Land no longer existed as a common wealth to meet the common needs of all the people. Land could now be owned. The owner could use the land in any way he desired, any way he thought might benefit himself. There was no longer any necessity to provide for the needs of others. Each person had his own little area."

"How did they pull that off?" Eloise James asked'

"They introduced money."

"Money?"

"Yes! Little pieces of paper that said they were worth something, that they represented a certain amount of property or some other good."

"You follow me? Whitney asked.

When Eloise nodded, Whitney continued: "Basically Europeans introduced debt ..."

"John Law!" blurted Eloise

"Oh yes! John Law. Of course he did not do it for the common good, out of a sense of the common wealth. He did it in order to make a profit."

"I don't understand how he pulled it off." Was the response of Eloise James.

"Guns."

"Guns???"

"Yes, he introduced guns. He sold the natives guns, twenty to thirty deerskins for one gun. The deer were no longer fellow creatures whose area had to be protected. They were now the price natives had to pay in order to get the guns they needed to destroy the deer."

"So it was no longer necessary to keep areas safe for the animals. They were now targets rather than fellow creatures." Eloise James interjected

"Exactly!" Without stopping Whitney continued: "The guns could kill the deer and other animals. But the guns also required ammunition. That ammunition also sold for twenty to thirty deerskins. Soon the deer were depleted and the Native Americans were in debt to the Europeans. We will take your land in payment of the debt they were told."

"The first debt was gun related" Eloise James said before she even realized what she was saying. When the full impact of her remark reached her brain Eloise added; "Not much has changed in a few hundred years." "Not much!" affirmed Whitney Thomas. He then reflects on the remarks of Pope Victor I. "The pope is correct. We have destroyed basic human relationships. We are definitely a disjointed society. We have separated ourselves from reality and history. We don't learn from past mistakes."

Eloise James nodded approvingly and Whitney concluded: "Our biggest mistakes is separating ourselves from the land and separating the land and the land owner. Although Pope Victor did not mention it explicitly our alienation began when the water, the earth, the air, the land, the trees, the heat from the sun were no longer our common wealth but could now be owned. The common wealth became the commonwealth. The state could now give out, dispense, and control these areas of our common wealth." Eloise James did not fully understand the distinction Whitney was proposing. that would come at a later time. Fortunately Eloise James did not think it was another story. Maybe another chapter but it WAS all one story.

Epilogue Restoring the Common WEALTH

In conclusion, I ask the reader to imagine. Imagine a world in which the Water, the Earth, the Air, the Land, the Trees, the Heat and light of the sun are a common WEALTH. No one may own or misuse them.

Imagine a world without money. BARTER GROUPS & COOPERATIVES are imagining such a world. Almost 40% of the U.S. population is engaged in barter or a cooperative group.

Imagine a world in which the food you eat is produced locally. If you check "farmers markets" on the internet you will find almost four million hits. So, almost 4 million GROUPS of people are imagining such a world.

Imagine a world in which land is owned locally and held in a common trust. Such imaginations exist in every state of the USA. There are close to 1000 such GROUPS of imaginers in the USA imagining such a world.

Imagine a world in which local businesses exist for the benefit of the local community. Members of the BUSINESS ALLIANCE FOR LOCAL LIVING ECONOMIES imagine such a world. These groups help promote sustainable agriculture, renewable energy and community capital.

Imagine a world in which the company's employees actually own the company for which they work. As more and more companies close in local communities the workers who would otherwise lose their jobs are finding ways to purchase such companies. There are people who are imagining such a world.

Imagine a world in which the state creates its own money and it is to be used for the benefit of its people. The people of North Dakota have been imagining it for one hundred years. The framers of the U.S. Constitution imagined such a world. North Dakota created its own state owned bank when the Federal Reserve was set up. As banks scoop more and more money from local economies more and more states are looking to set up a similar bank.

Imagine a world without nuclear weapons. The members of MAYORS FOR PEACE are and have been imagining it. Over 5000 mayors world-wide have joined an effort to eliminate all nuclear weapons by 2020.

Imagine a world in which there is no war. Quaker groups have been imagining such a world for a long time. Pax Christi members are imagining it. Many other pacifist groups are imaging it.

Imagine a world without the death penalty. Helen Prejean is imagining it. There are vigils at state capitals whenever people are executed. Obviously Helen Prejean is not the only one imagining such a world. The others haven't written books and inspired movies yet. But they are out there.

The most basic imagination is the first one mentioned. Imagine a world in which the Water, the Earth, the Air, the Land, the Trees, the Heat and light of the sun are a common WEALTH. No one may own or misuse them. The people of ESTONIA are imagining such a world. Once the Soviet Union was dissolved Estonia declared that the State owned all the natural resources, the banks and money - in short, everything necessary for survival of the people. No one may misuse them.

The people of BOLIVIA imagine such a world. In December 2011 Bolivia passed a law: all natural elements Water Earth Air Land Trees etc. have an <u>inherent</u> right to life. No one may infringe on that right.

None of these imagining would be original. In fact it is the most ancient of imaginings. It is the imagination of the creator. Once I realized that I did not have to present a new imagination, I simply had to be faithful to the creator's imagination then I realized I did not have to talk so much. I simply had to be faithful to the creator's original thought. I have presented you with just a few of today's imaginers. This book is simply an attempt to be faithful to the creator's imagination. It is not necessary to list all of today's imaginers. There are many people today being faithful to that imagination? Can you please give us a hand?